W9-CCN-456

JELLYFISH

by Katie Marsico

Children's Press®

An Imprint of Scholastic Inc.
New York Toronto London Auckland Sydney
Mexico City New Delhi Hong Kong
Danbury, Connecticut

Content Consultant
Dr. Stephen S. Ditchkoff
Professor of Wildlife Sciences
Auburn University
Auburn, Alabama

Photographs ©: Alamy Images/WorldFoto: 36; Animals Animals/ Ardea/Ken Lucas: 19; Dreamstime: 5 bottom, 39 (Climberjk), 20, 21 (Richard Mcmillin), 1, 22, 23 (Sieber), 11 (Svetlana Foote), 2, 3, 14, 15, 46 (Vilainecrevette); Getty Images: 40, 41 (Valery Hache), cover (Yomiuri Shimbun/AFP); Minden Pictures/David Shale: 35; Shutterstock, Inc./rangizzz: 2 background, 3 background, 44 background, 45 background; Superstock, Inc.: 8, 9 (Biosphoto), 5 top, 24, 25 (Marka), 7, 26, 27, 31 (Minden Pictures), 16, 17 (NHPA), 28, 29 (Norbert Wu), 4, 5, 12, 13 (Reinhard Dirscherl/Mauritius); Thinkstock/KonovalikovAndrey: 32, 33.

Map by Bob Italiano

Library of Congress Cataloging-in-Publication Data
Marsico, Katie, 1980– author.
Jellyfish / by Katie Marsico.
pages cm. — (Nature's children)
Audience: Ages 9–12.
Audience: Grades 4 to 6.
Includes bibliographical references and index.
ISBN 978-0-531-20664-5 (lib. bdg.) —
ISBN 978-0-531-21657-6 (pbk.)
1. Jellyfishes—Juvenile literature. I. Title. II. Series: Nature's children (New York, N.Y.)
QL377.S4N265 2014
593.5'3—dc23 2014001511

Printed in China 62

1 2 3 4 5 6 7 8 9 10 R 24 23 22 21 20 19 18 17 16 15

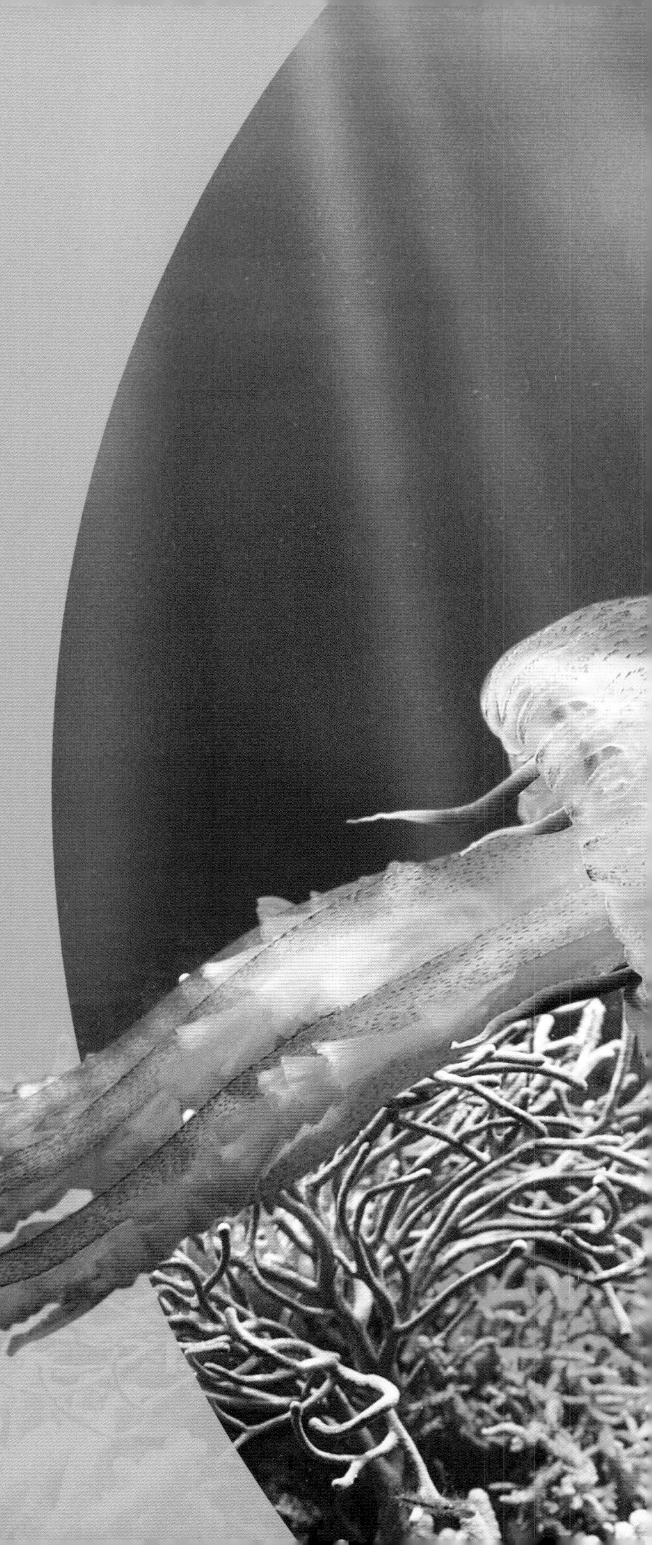

FACT FILE

Jellyfish

Class	Scyphozoa
Order	Coronatae, Rhizostomeae, and Semaeostomeae
Families	19 total, including Atollidae, Cassiopeidae, Cyaneidae, and Ulmaridae
Genera	58 total, including *Atolla*, *Aurelia*, *Cassiopea*, and *Cyanea*
Species	Roughly 200 total, including *Atolla wyvillei*, *Aurelia aurita*, *Cassiopea xamachana*, and *Cyanea capillata*
World distribution	All major world oceans
Habitat	Shallow coastal environments but also areas as deep as 12,000 feet (3.7 kilometers) beneath the surface; locations with varying water temperatures
Distinctive physical characteristics	Adults in medusa phase are colorless or shades of blue, brown, or pink; simple body plan includes parts that stretch outward from a central point; skin is usually transparent and thin; juveniles in polyp phase have a cylinder-shaped stalk body with tentacles
Habits	Adults in medusa phase sometimes have symbiotic relationships with other sea animals; can be solitary or members of large groups called smacks; reproduce sexually; sweep food into their mouth or stun and trap prey using tentacles; juveniles in polyp phase are capable of asexual reproduction; often live attached to other polyps as members of a larger colony
Diet	Adults in medusa phase feed mostly on zooplankton but also eat small crabs, fish, and sometimes other jellyfish; adults in juvenile polyp phase feed mainly on zooplankton

JELLYFISH

Contents

CHAPTER 1

Floating Phantoms

Sunlight sparkles across the warm waters of the Gulf of Mexico. Life is quiet in the middle of the open ocean. Occasionally, the stillness is briefly interrupted by a passing boat or leaping dolphin.

However, the sea's surface is actually being stirred by more movement than meets the eye. A closer look reveals what appear to be hundreds of eerie bubbles. These saucer-shaped ghosts slowly bob back and forth with the rhythm of the waves. Are they alive? Yes! They're remarkable and mysterious animals called moon jellies.

Moon jellies are an example of what scientists call true jellyfish. Other types of sea life have jellylike characteristics. True jellyfish are described as free-swimming **invertebrates** that have a soft, rounded body as adults. True jellyfish also sport **tentacles** that contain stinging **cells** capable of causing painful and sometimes dangerous wounds. This is one of the reasons they are both fascinating and feared.

Alaska's Kinak Bay is home to moon jellies.

Where Jellyfish Are Found

Jellyfish live in every ocean around the world. They live in icy Antarctic waters and warm tropical seas such as the Caribbean. These marine animals are able to tolerate a wide variety of water temperatures.

Jellyfish exist in a broad range of individual **habitats** as well. Most **species** are found in shallow coastal **environments**. However, some jellyfish live in deep, dark areas that reach as far as 12,000 feet (3.7 kilometers) beneath the waves!

Most of a jellyfish's time is spent drifting through the water. **Currents** play a large part in determining the speed and direction of a jellyfish's movement. Jellyfish are often spotted slowly bobbing near the ocean's surface in large groups. Sometimes storms or rough waves cause them to wash ashore. Unfortunately, these delicate invertebrates can't move on land and are unable to survive more than a few hours out of water.

Dead zones in the Pacific Ocean are so polluted that the only thing that can live there are jellyfish.

A Range of Appearances

In the water, jellyfish frequently have a strange appearance. The soft, rounded part of a jellyfish's body is called the bell or umbrella. It is usually **transparent** and shaped like a bell or saucer. In most cases, long, thin tentacles dangle from its bottom.

Jellyfish range in size and color. Depending on the species, the **diameter** of the bell can measure anywhere from less than 1 inch (2.5 centimeters) to 12 feet (3.7 meters). Some jellyfish are different shades of pink, blue, or brown. Others have virtually no color at all.

A jellyfish's body is simple. It does not have a brain, heart, or bones. Jellyfish have a main cavity, or hollow space, where digestion occurs. A single orifice, or opening, is used to take in food and remove waste. These animals also have **radial symmetry**. In other words, their body parts are similar to the spokes on a wheel. They all stretch outward from a central point.

Many jellyfish have transparent bells, making it easy to observe the insides of their bodies.

CHAPTER 2

Built for Survival

Jellyfish aren't complex animals. Yet they have survived for hundreds of millions of years, thanks to several amazing physical features. For starters, a jellyfish's physical makeup allows it to easily float. This is because about 90 to 95 percent of its body is water.

Most jellyfish don't simply lie motionless as currents carry them across the waves. They move through the water with an up-and-down rhythm. They sink and rise by contracting, or tightening, a ring of muscle around their bell. This squeezing motion closes the bell and pushes water out of the jellyfish. The result is that the jellyfish shoots forward. Eventually, it relaxes its muscles, causing the bell to reopen and refill with water.

Since a jellyfish's movements are subtle, they often aren't obvious to **predators**. Tuna, sharks, swordfish, salmon, and sea turtles feed on these invertebrates. Sometimes different species of jellyfish also eat each other.

Sea turtles can be a threat to even very large jellyfish.

Terrific Tentacles

Jellyfish are largely filter feeders. As they swim, they strain tiny food particles from the water. They use their tentacles to sweep prey, or pieces of prey, into their mouth. Depending on the species, a jellyfish's diet might include small fish, crabs, zooplankton, or even other jellyfish.

Not all jellyfish have the same number of tentacles. Some have just a few, while others have more than 800. Tentacles vary in size as well. They can measure less than 1 inch (2.5 cm) long or stretch to lengths of about 120 feet (37 m). That's roughly the height of a 10-story building!

A jellyfish has four to eight shorter, thicker tentacles near its mouth. These are called oral arms. Jellyfish rely on their longer tentacles to collect food from the water. They depend on their oral arms to guide the food to their mouth.

Jellyfish often have oral arms that are much smaller than their main tentacles.

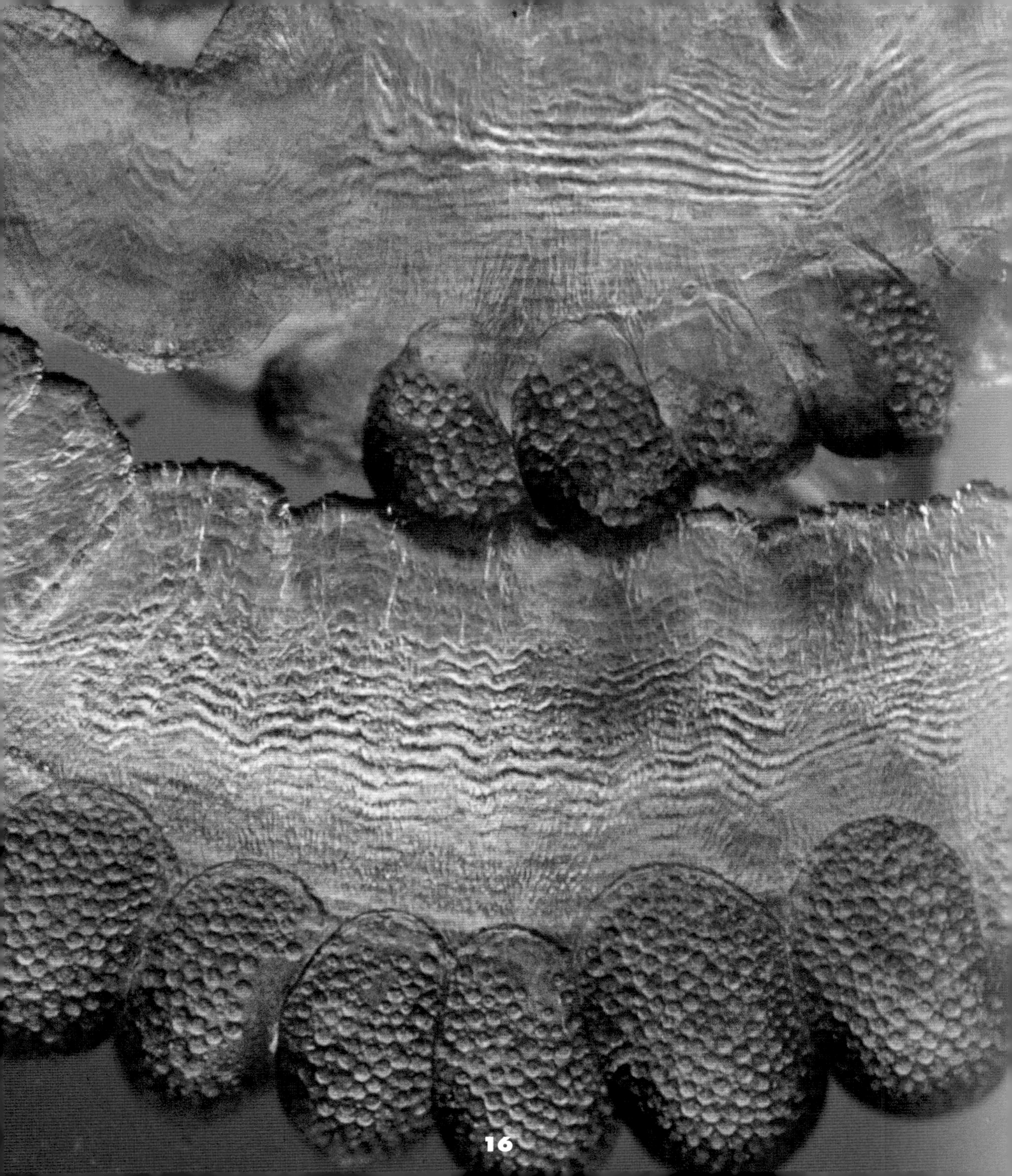

A Stunning Sting

A jellyfish's tentacles aren't just used for filter feeding. These animals often rely on their long, flexible arms to attack larger prey. Jellyfish tentacles are capable of packing a painful punch because they contain stinging cells called nematocysts.

Nematocysts are extremely sensitive to touch. They break open when they brush against something in the water. When nematocysts burst, they release a tiny, **venom**-filled barb, or pointy spine. The barb pierces whatever the jellyfish's tentacles have come into contact with. In many cases, this happens to be the flesh of prey. The poison in the barb stuns or kills the unlucky animal. This makes it easier for the jellyfish to pull its meal toward its mouth.

Stinging tentacles also help defend against enemies. However, jellyfish can't tell the difference between swimmers and potential predators. As a result, people sometimes get stung by jellyfish barbs. These wounds can be painful but are usually not life threatening.

A single tentacle (magnified at left) contains many nematocysts.

A Look at Body Layers

Jellyfish don't have a complicated digestive system. Their mouth leads directly to their stomach cavity, which is lined by an inner layer of cells. This is where **nutrients** are absorbed.

A thick, jellylike substance lies between a jellyfish's inner cells and its outer body surface. This middle layer is called the mesoglea. It typically contains nerves and muscles. It also provides physical support in place of bones and a skeleton. The mesoglea is fairly elastic. It helps a jellyfish return to its original shape after the animal contracts its muscles to swim.

The invertebrate's outer layer of skin is extremely thin. This allows jellyfish to absorb oxygen without actually breathing. In addition, extra oxygen is stored in the mesoglea. The result is that jellyfish can tolerate water with low oxygen levels. Other animals that lack similar features might struggle to survive in the same environments.

A jellyfish's mouth is located on the underside of its bell.

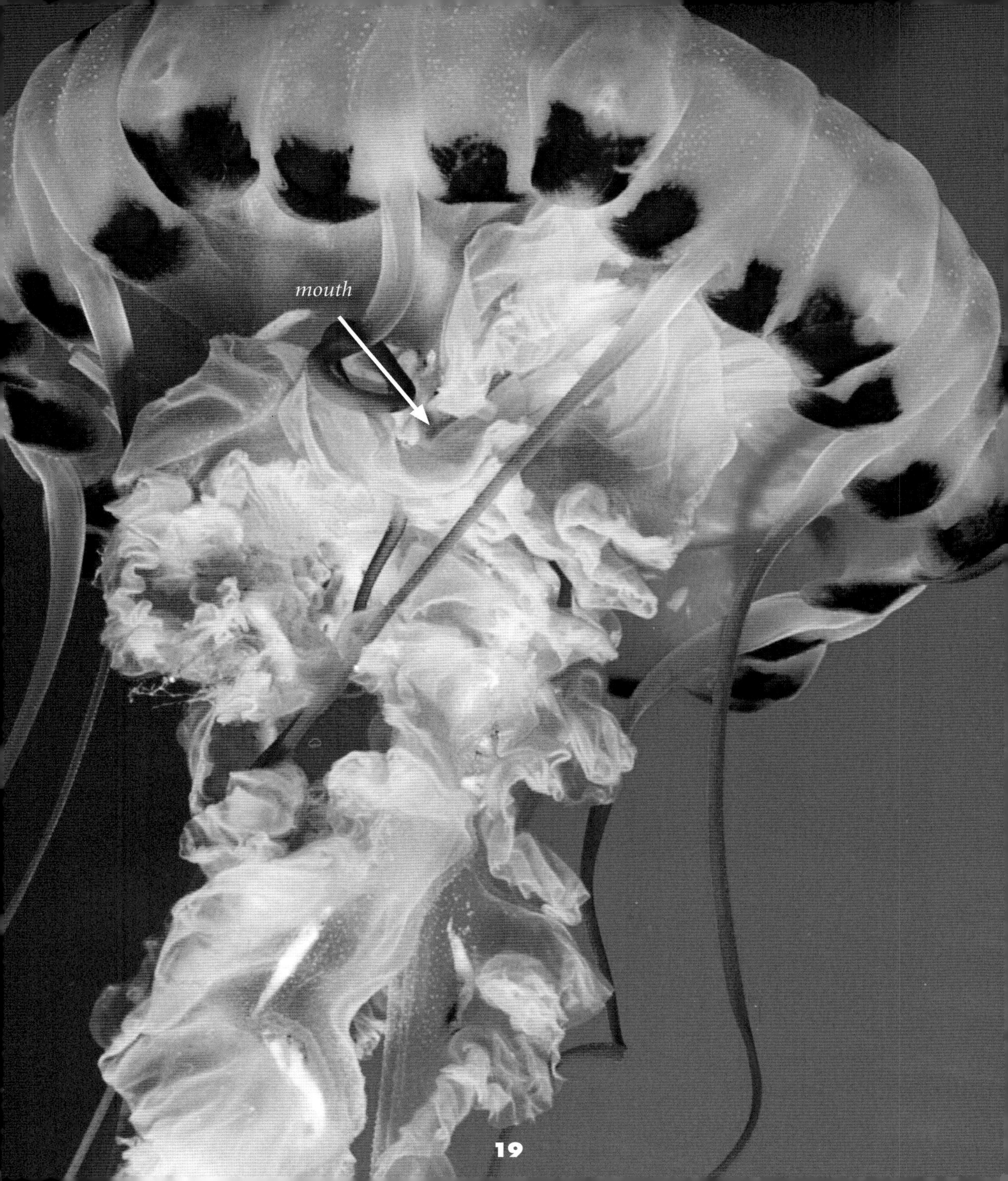
mouth

Blending in and Being a Partner

Camouflage is another physical trait that jellyfish rely on for survival. Being transparent allows these marine animals to blend in with the water around them. Some jellyfish are also bioluminescent. This means that, like fireflies, their bodies produce chemicals that react to create a light display. Scientists suspect that jellyfish mainly use bioluminescence to startle or confuse predators.

In certain cases, jellyfish share a symbiotic relationship with other sea animals. For instance, some fish are unaffected by a jellyfish's poisonous sting. They are able to take shelter near or within its tentacles. Such fish frequently feed on whatever the jellyfish eats. Sometimes these fish provide the jellyfish with protection against predators. Other times, the fish serve as bait. They attract animals that the jellyfish then traps with its tentacles.

FUN FACT! Jellyfish aren't the only animals that light up the water! Scientists estimate that about 90 percent of the sea life in the deepest parts of the ocean are bioluminescent.

Bioluminescent jellyfish light up some of the world's darkest, deepest waters.

Useful Sensory Cells

Jellyfish don't process information the same way as animals that have a brain. Instead, they depend on a network of nerves to react to the world around them. Certain species have more powerful sensory systems than others.

For example, some jellyfish have eyespots. These spots are found in pockets along the edge of the bell. They aren't really eyes, but they are sensitive to changes in light. As a result, eyespots guide jellyfish as they swim. They might even be a way for jellyfish to determine the location of predators and prey.

Other sensory cells help jellyfish detect chemicals related to taste and smell. Scientists believe they're probably used to find food. A jellyfish also relies on sensory cells to stay balanced. If it tips too much to one side, various nerve endings cause the invertebrate's muscles to contract. This allows the jellyfish to right itself.

Though jellyfish do not have eyes, they are able to sense certain visual changes in their environment.

CHAPTER 3

A Look at a Life Cycle

Jellyfish do not have a very long life span. In fact, most live less than one year. Certain species don't even survive more than a few days.

Though a jellyfish's life is brief, its life cycle is still complex. These animals often take a few different physical forms between birth and death. People are usually most familiar with the last one. It is called the medusa stage. This is when a jellyfish is able to swim freely and has a bell and tentacles that dangle in the water.

The name medusa refers to a creature from ancient Greek mythology. The Greeks thought Medusa had snakes for hair. They also believed she could turn people into stone simply by staring at them. Of course, jellyfish don't have hair or actual eyes. But they do have snakelike tentacles that they use to stun and kill prey.

A medusa is a fully grown adult jellyfish.

The Earliest Stage

Depending on the species, jellyfish in the medusa stage can either be solitary or live in large groups called smacks. Particularly dense smacks have been known to include millions of animals and cover more than 100 miles (161 km) of coastline. When this many jellyfish come together at once, it is called a bloom. Scientists believe blooms are probably related to sexual reproduction.

After sexual reproduction, females store eggs either in their stomach or in pouches along their oral arms. Eventually, larvae known as planulae hatch from the eggs. Most people would not necessarily recognize that the planulae are young jellyfish. These oval-shaped larvae lack tentacles. Instead, they are lined with tiny hairs called cilia. When the cilia flap together, they move the planulae short distances through the water.

At first, the planulae float near the ocean's surface. After a few days, they drop downward. Planulae frequently attach to rocks and shells on the seafloor.

Planulae lack the distinctive body shape of the medusa.

From Polyp to Medusa

Jellyfish planulae gradually develop a mouth and early tentacles. They use the tentacles to obtain food. By this point, they have entered the next stage in their life cycle and are considered polyps.

Jellyfish polyps look like cylinder-shaped stalks. They are capable of asexual reproduction. This means they don't need a male or female partner to multiply. New polyps simply bud from older polyps.

Over time, **colonies** of attached polyps develop along the ocean floor. A colony often resembles a grooved stack of saucers. Ultimately, the top layer of the stack detaches. This marks the beginning of the ephyra stage.

An ephyra is basically a small, free-swimming jellyfish with tentacles. It grows until it reaches the medusa phase and is able to sexually reproduce. Soon, a new wave of animals experiences the incredible journey that shapes a jellyfish's life cycle.

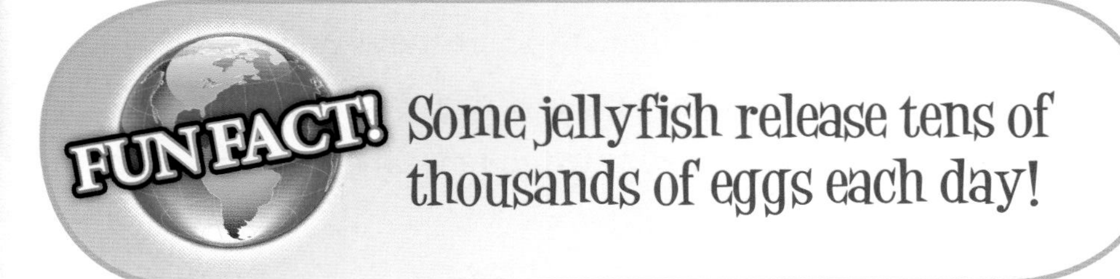

Polyps have smaller tentacles than medusas.

CHAPTER 4

Prehistory and the Present

Scientists often figure out how long certain animals have been on Earth by studying their fossils, or hardened remains. Jellyfish fossils are quite rare, though. This is because little is left behind when they and other soft-bodied invertebrates die. Fortunately, the rare fossils that are discovered offer valuable clues about how long jellyfish have existed.

Most experts think that jellyfish were floating in Earth's seas long before dinosaurs roamed the planet. Fossils suggest that jellyfish appeared about 650 million years ago. Dinosaurs followed roughly 420 million years later.

Fossils also reveal that the first jellyfish looked remarkably similar to today's species. They had a bell-shaped body with tentacles. In addition, these prehistoric creatures moved and obtained food much the same way that their modern relatives do. As time passed, jellyfish adjusted to new environments and developed into different species.

These 150-million-year-old jellyfish fossils were discovered in Germany.

Examining the Jellyfish Identity

Scientists use a system called taxonomy to divide plants and animals into different groups. A phylum is one example of such a group. Animals within a phylum share the same general body plan.

Jellyfish are part of the phylum Cnidaria. Cnidarians all have radial symmetry and a saclike inner body cavity. Corals, sea anemones, and hydras are also members of this phylum.

Yet jellyfish belong to their own class called Scyphozos. The term *Scyphozoa* traces back to the Greek word *skyphos*, which means "cup." This name refers to the cuplike shape of a jellyfish's bell.

Scientists first described jellyfish as scyphozoans in 1887. Approximately 200 species make up this class of free-swimming marine invertebrates. At some point in their life cycle, all scyphozoans go through a medusa stage during which they have a jellylike body. Experts currently recognize three orders of Scyphozoa: crown jellyfish, flag-mouth jellyfish, and root-mouth jellyfish.

Like jellyfish, sea anemones have a wide range of colors.

A Sampling of Species

Crown jellyfish have a grooved bell, which some people compare to the shape of a crown. Scientists still have much to learn about these jellyfish, since they often exist in deep-sea environments. One example of a crown jellyfish is the bioluminescent *Atolla*. It is found in the Atlantic, Pacific, and Arctic Oceans, as well as in the Gulf of Mexico.

Flag-mouth species such as the lion's mane jellyfish have large tentacles and four long, frilly oral arms. The lion's mane lives in cooler parts of the Atlantic and Pacific. With tentacles measuring up to 120 feet (37 m) long, it is the world's largest jellyfish.

The upside-down jellyfish also swims through the Atlantic and Pacific, as well as the Mediterranean Sea. It belongs to the root-mouth order. These animals have no tentacles hanging from their bell. Instead, they possess just eight oral arms that are fused, or joined together. Each arm has tiny openings that suck up food and water like the roots of a plant do.

Atolla *jellyfish are bright red.*

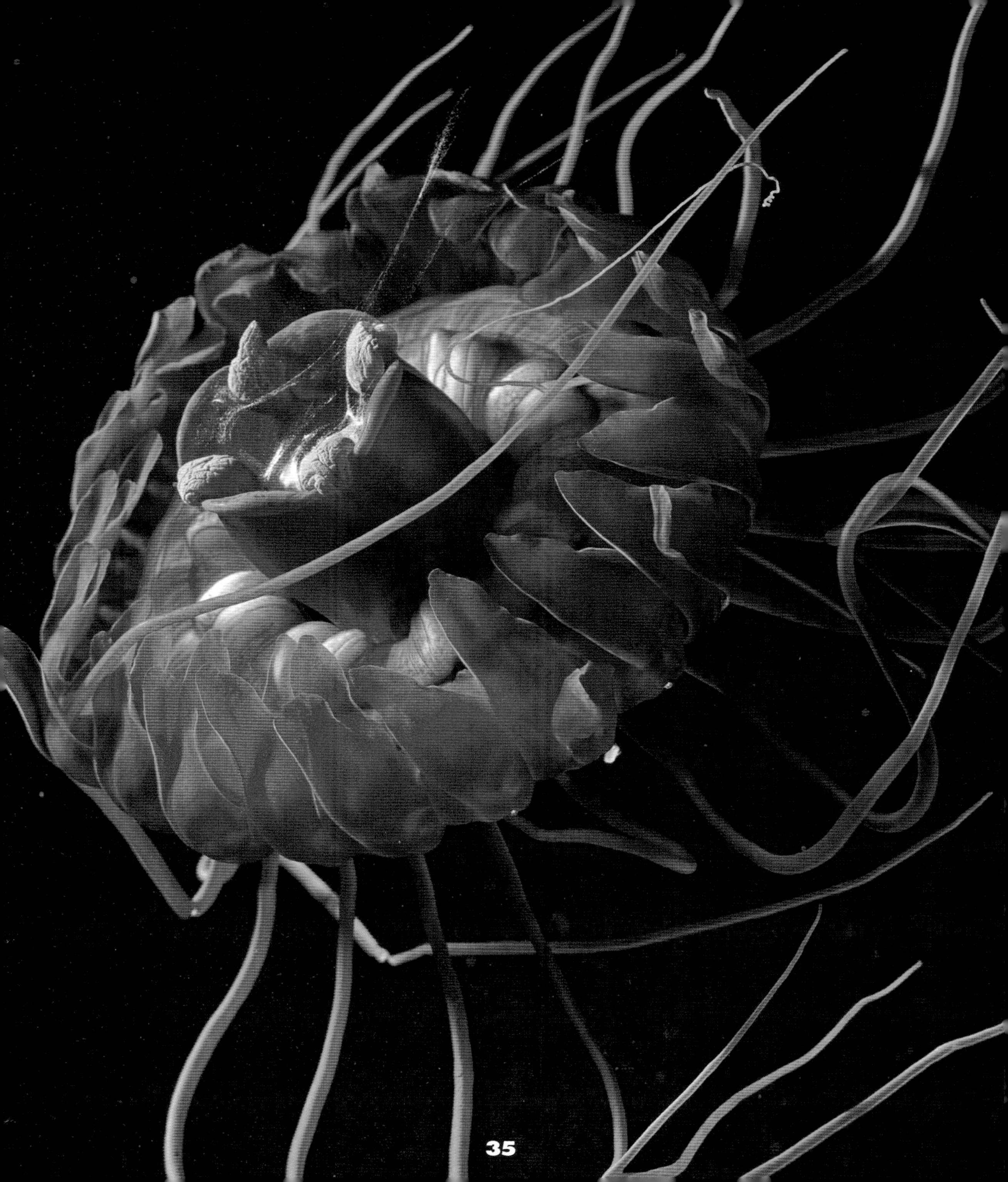

What's in a Name?

For such a simple creature, there are several complicated issues surrounding how jellyfish are named. Sometimes the terms *jellyfish* and *jelly* are used interchangeably. This is not always correct. All jellyfish are jellies, but not all jellies are jellyfish.

The name *jellies* also applies to comb jellies, which belong to a completely separate phylum from jellyfish. Both animals share some physical similarities. Many comb jellies even have a pair of non-stinging tentacles. But they are better known for their fused cilia. These connected hairs are called combs. Comb jellies rely on their combs to move through the water.

The confusion doesn't end there. Most scientists agree that scyphozoans are the only true jellyfish. Nevertheless, cnidarians include several jellyfish look-alikes. Some animals are labeled "jellyfish" but either aren't free-swimming or don't experience a significant medusa phase. Others, such as box jellyfish, have more highly developed nervous systems than scyphozoans.

Because of its body shape, the the box jellyfish is often mistaken for a true jellyfish.

CHAPTER 5

Sharing the Sea

Humans and jellyfish share a challenging relationship. Even though few people die from the venom in jellyfish tentacles, no one enjoys being stung. In addition, jellyfish blooms appear to be on the rise. Scientists believe this is due to overfishing, pollution, and changes in water temperature. All of these factors create favorable conditions for jellyfish reproduction.

Unfortunately, the results of jellyfish blooms often go far beyond an occasional sting. They have a negative effect on commercial fishing because the jellyfish can clog nets. Tourism is also impacted when blooms sweep past popular beaches.

At the same time, it is dangerous to dismiss jellyfish as pests that deserve to be wiped off the planet. Many animals, including **endangered** sea turtles, depend on them as a food source. In addition, scientists still have much to learn about jellyfish, especially those that live in the deep sea.

Signs are sometimes posted at beaches to warn people that jellyfish are present.

STINGERS
MARINE STINGERS
ARE PRESENT IN
THESE WATERS
DURING THE SUMMER
MONTHS

22qt.
20L
20qt.
15L
16qt.
12qt.
10L
8qt.
5L
4qt.
VITLAB
simplex

Improving the Outlook

Conservationists are working to find new ways for humans and jellyfish to share Earth's oceans and seas. These animals offer important clues about the health of their environment. For example, the recent increase in blooms could mean that jellyfish predators are being overhunted. It may also serve as a warning that people need to do a better job of keeping the water clean.

Tackling bigger environmental issues is just one way to improve humans' relationship with jellyfish. Educating the public is another. Scientists continue to raise awareness about avoiding and treating jellyfish stings. Beachgoers should always pay attention to signs and bulletins to steer clear of areas where blooms are occurring.

Jellyfish have been bobbing across the waves much longer than people have been swimming. These graceful and misunderstood creatures have managed to outlive animals that have brains and far more complex bodies. Jellyfish deserve humans' respect, as well as the opportunity to exist alongside us for many years to come.

Researchers collect jellyfish samples so they can study the animals more closely in laboratories.

Words to Know

camouflage (KAM-uh-flahzh) — a disguise or a natural coloring that allows animals, people, or objects to hide by making them look like their surroundings

cells (SELZ) — the smallest units of animals or plants

class (KLAS) — in taxonomy, a group of related plants or animals that is larger than an order but smaller than a phylum

colonies (KAH-luh-neez) — large groups of animals that live together

conservationists (kon-sur-VAY-shun-ists) — people who work to protect an environment and the living things in it

currents (KUR-uhnts) — movements of water in a definite direction in a river or an ocean

diameter (dye-AM-uh-tur) — a straight line passing through the center of a circle, connecting opposite sides

endangered (en-DAYN-jurd) — at risk of becoming extinct, usually because of human activity

environments (en-VYE-ruhn-muhnts) — the natural surroundings of living things, such as the air, land, or sea

habitats (HAB-uh-tats) — the places where an animal or a plant is usually found

invertebrates (in-VUR-tuh-brits) — animals without a backbone

larvae (LAR-vee) — a jellyfish's immature form before a period of major physical change and development

nutrients (NOO-tree-uhnts) — substances such as proteins, minerals, or vitamins that are needed by people, animals, and plants to stay strong and healthy

orders (OR-durz) — groups of related plants or animals that are bigger than a family but smaller than a class

predators (PRED-uh-turz) — animals that live by hunting other animals for food

prey (PRAY) — an animal hunted by another animal for food

radial symmetry (RAY-dee-uhl SIH-muh-tree) — the condition of having similar body parts arranged around a central point, like the spokes on a wheel

sensory (SEN-sur-ee) — having to do with an animal's senses, such as the sense of touch and the sense of feeling

sexual reproduction (SEK-shoo-uhl ree-pruh-DUHK-shuhn) — the process of mating to create new life

solitary (SAH-luh-ter-ee) — not requiring or without the companionship of others

species (SPEE-sheez) — one of the groups into which animals and plants of the same genus are divided; members of the same species can mate and have offspring

symbiotic (sim-bee-AH-tik) — a type of relationship in which two different kinds of life-forms live together and depend on one another

tentacles (TEN-tuh-kuhlz) — long, flexible limbs that are used for moving, feeling, and grasping

transparent (trans-PAIR-uhnt) — letting light through so that objects on the other side can be seen clearly

venom (VEN-uhm) — poison produced by some animals

Habitat Map

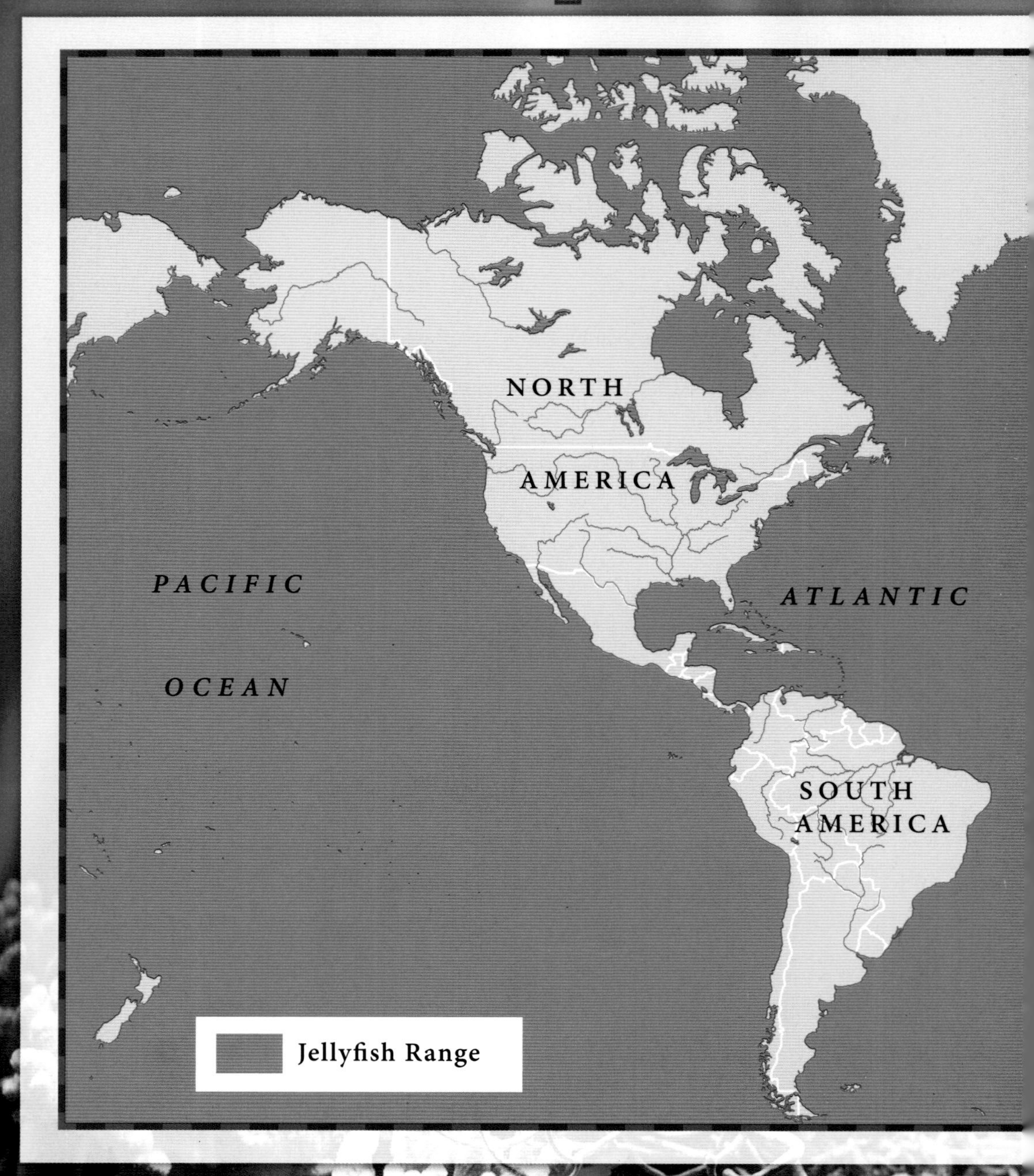
NORTH
AMERICA
PACIFIC
OCEAN
ATLANTIC
SOUTH
AMERICA
Jellyfish Range